Where's That Fish?

by Barbara Brenner and Bernice Chardiet
Illustrated by Carol Schwartz

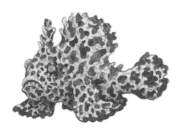

Cartwheel
B·O·O·K·S®

SCHOLASTIC INC.

NEW YORK   TORONTO   LONDON   AUCKLAND   SYDNEY

ISBN 0-590-45215-0

Text copyright © 1994 by Barbara Brenner and Bernice Chardiet.
Published by arrangement with Chardiet Unlimited, Inc.
Illustrations copyright © 1994 by Carol Schwartz.
All rights reserved. Published by Scholastic Inc.
CARTWHEEL BOOKS is a registered trademark of Scholastic Inc.
HIDE & SEEK SCIENCE is a trademark of Chardiet Unlimited, Inc.

12 11 10 9 8 7 6 5   4 5 6 7 8 9/9

Printed in the U.S.A.   09

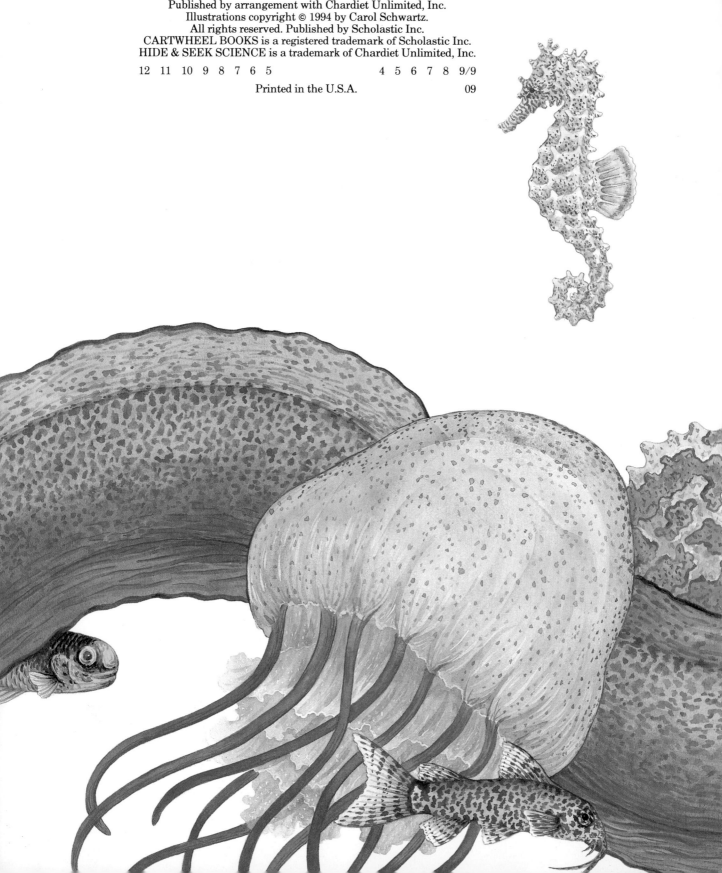

Introduction

Come on! Jump in!
You won't get wet!
You don't even
Need a net!

Find the red fish
And the blue fish.
Find the "jellies,"
Are they true fish?

See the swimmers
Big and small.
If you look sharp,
You'll find them all.

Clown Fish Hideout

There's always danger on the coral reef! But the little clown fish has found a safe place to hide. It is resting in a sea anemone (uh-NEM-uh-nee) — an underwater creature that looks like a flower. Do you see the clown face peeking out?

It's a Fact:
The stinging arms of sea anemones usually mean death for little fish. But this clown fish is safe. It is a special clown fish that the anemone will not harm. Why is the anemone not harmful to this special fish? Scientists are working on that mystery!

Crazy Catfish!

Here's an underwater crowd scene. Can you find the catfish? They're the fish with "whiskers." Look at that! One of them is upside down.

It's a Fact:
There are many different kinds of catfish. Most of them have cat-like whiskers called barbels, which help the catfish find food. There are more than one thousand kinds of catfish — including the upside-down catfish!

Something Fishy!

These fish are snacking on underwater weeds. But wait! There's something fishy here! One of these weed-covered rocks is really a frogfish! It's lying in wait to suck those fish into its big mouth. Which one of the rocks is a frogfish? (*Hint:* Look for two blue eyes.)

It's a Fact:
Frogfish rarely swim. They lie on the bottom of the ocean and wait for food. When they do move, they hop along using their fins. Now can you guess why they're called frogfish?

Seahorse Nursery

A head like a horse. A tail like a monkey.
A pouch like a kangaroo. Is it a fish? Yes!
It's called a seahorse. Somewhere in this
scene, you can see five of them — two
full-grown seahorses and three babies.
Can you find them all?

It's a Fact:
Among seahorses, it's the father
who has the babies. The female
lays the eggs in the male's pouch.
The male carries the eggs and
gives birth to the young.
Seahorse babies are about as big
as your thumbnail.

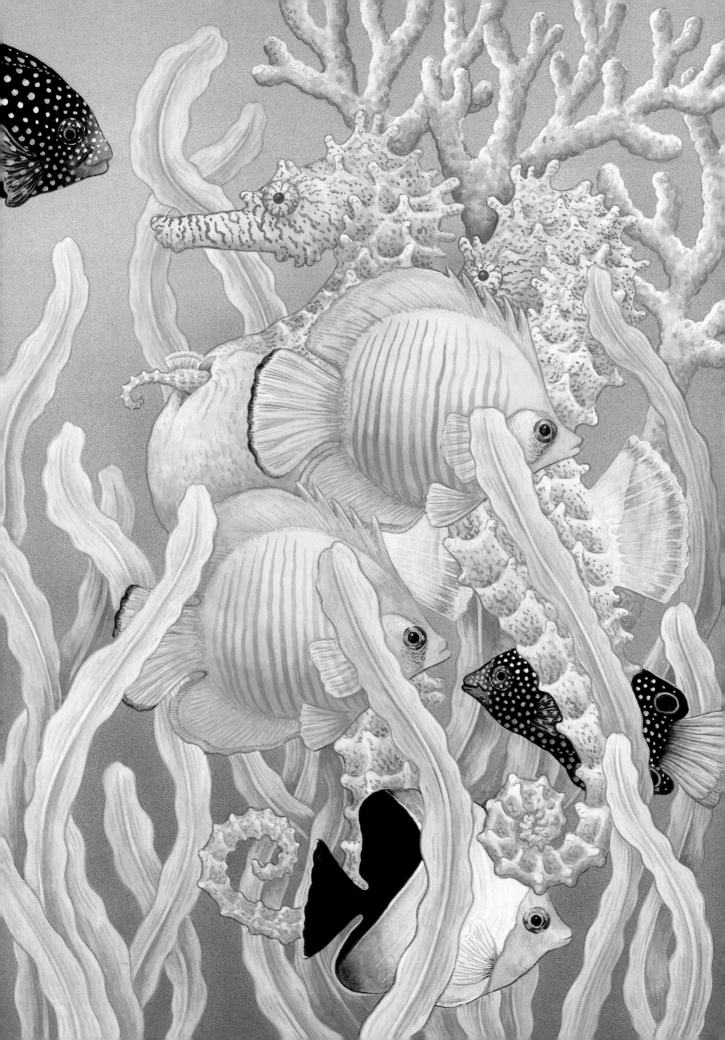

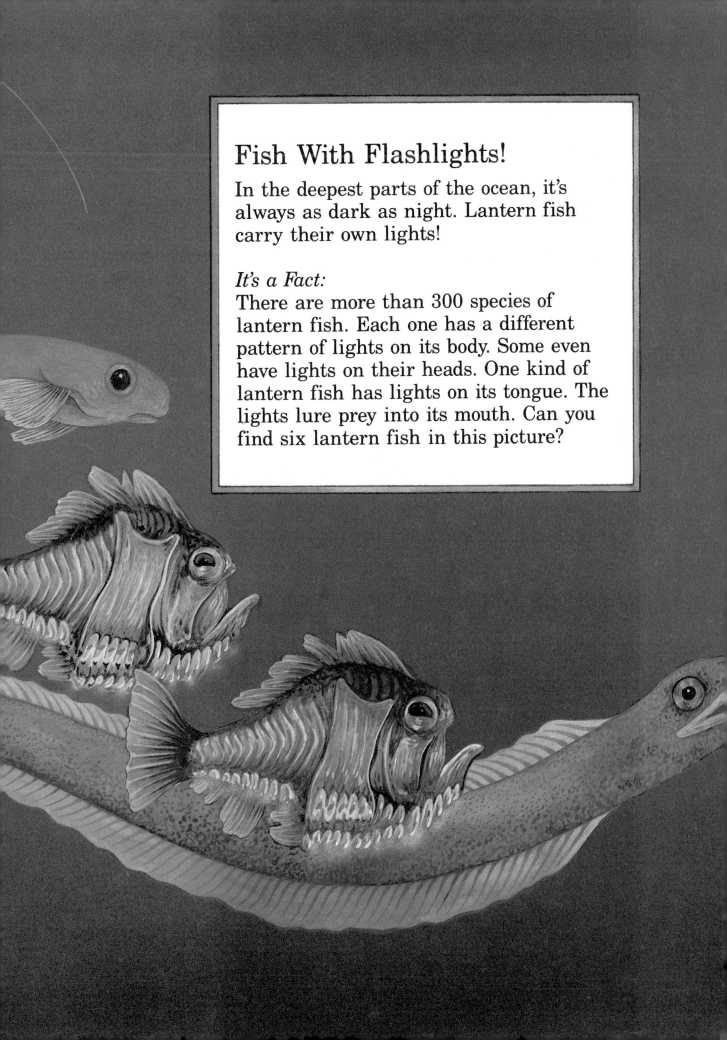

Fish With Flashlights!

In the deepest parts of the ocean, it's always as dark as night. Lantern fish carry their own lights!

It's a Fact:
There are more than 300 species of lantern fish. Each one has a different pattern of lights on its body. Some even have lights on their heads. One kind of lantern fish has lights on its tongue. The lights lure prey into its mouth. Can you find six lantern fish in this picture?

Sneaky Starfish

The starfish preys on many creatures of the sea. Somewhere in this picture a starfish is sneaking up on a scallop. The scallop has lots of eyes. Maybe it will see the starfish. Do you?

It's a Fact:
Starfish come in many colors and sizes.
You can sometimes find them on the
beach. Their arms grab and hold prey.
If a starfish loses one of its arms,
another one will grow in its place.

A Jewel of a Fish

Jewel fish are known for their beautiful colors. No two are exactly alike, as you can see. In this scene, you'll find nine jewel fish — all different. You'll also find one lone zebra fish that's hiding.

It's a Fact:
The zebra fish is smart to hide. Jewel fish are bullies. They attack other fish. If you have a home aquarium, don't put other kinds of fish in with a jewel fish.

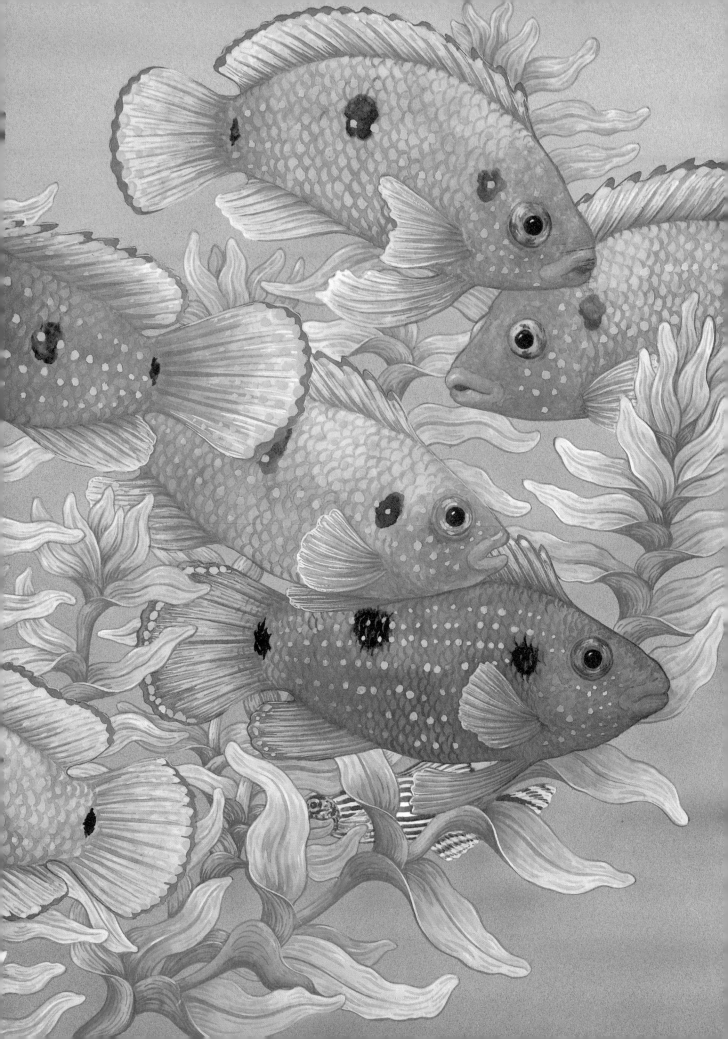

Did You Ever See a Swimming Leaf?

Here's a quiet freshwater pond with fish swimming and dead leaves floating in it. But which is which? Leaf fish look a lot like floating leaves. Which are the leaves? Which are the fish?

It's a Fact:
Leaf fish drift slowly through the water with their heads pointed downward. Their eyes and fins blend with their colors. Some even have a little "stem" hanging from their mouths! Leaf fish are big eaters. A tiny leaf fish will eat its own weight in food every day.

Cave Monster!

Sea creatures, beware! A moray eel is lurking in this coral cave. Can you see its spotted head? If it strikes, its whole body will come snaking out of its hiding place. It has big teeth and sometimes bites people. Quick! Find this monster!

It's a Fact:
Some moray eels are striped like zebras. Others have spots or bright colors. They breathe with their mouths open, so they look as if they are about to bite!

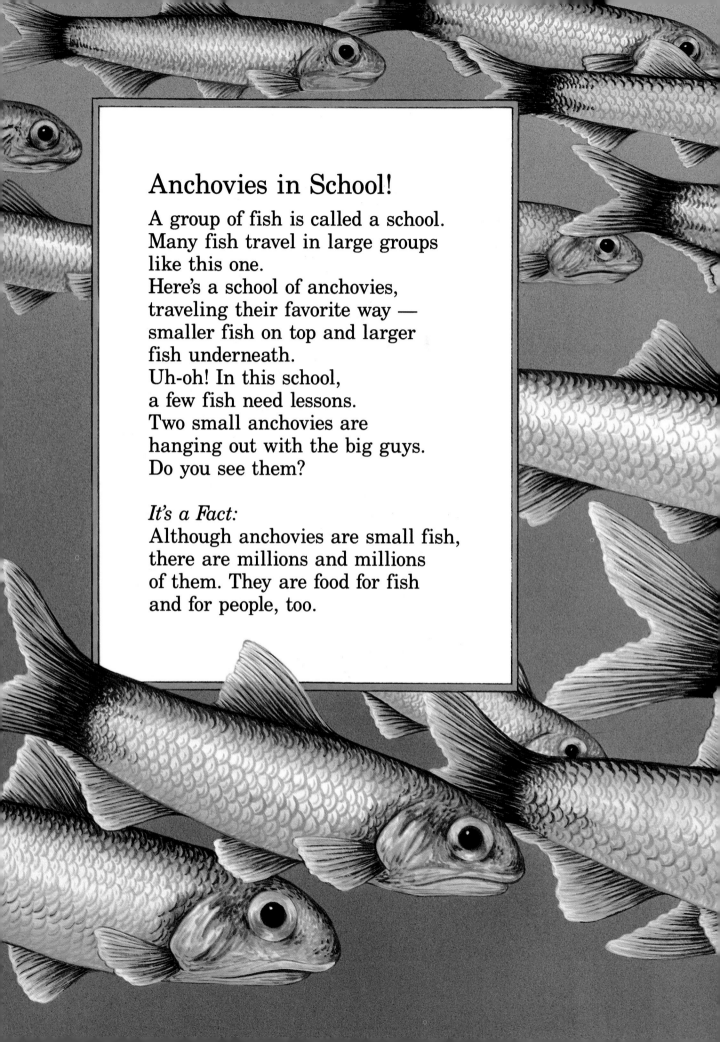

Anchovies in School!

A group of fish is called a school.
Many fish travel in large groups
like this one.
Here's a school of anchovies,
traveling their favorite way —
smaller fish on top and larger
fish underneath.
Uh-oh! In this school,
a few fish need lessons.
Two small anchovies are
hanging out with the big guys.
Do you see them?

It's a Fact:
Although anchovies are small fish,
there are millions and millions
of them. They are food for fish
and for people, too.

Goldfish, Goldfish Everywhere

Here's a tank that holds many different varieties of goldfish. One of the fish has eyes at the top of its head. It can't see you. But can you see it?

It's a Fact:
Goldfish can be blue, green, black, brown, yellow, or white, as well as orange. The fish with its eyes toward the sky is called a celestial goldfish. People have been breeding goldfish for more than a thousand years. That's why there are so many varieties.

Jellyfish Jamboree

These jellyfish moving through the water
look like little umbrellas made of jelly.
They're all different. The smallest is a
sea wasp. It's about the size of a grape.
Its tentacles can sting and kill its prey.
Can you find the sea wasp?

It's a Fact:
Some jellyfish are blue; others are pink,
violet, brown, or other colors. All jellyfish
have long poisonous tentacles with which
they kill their prey.

MALE   FEMALE

Guppies Galore!

Here are a male and a female guppy.
Would you believe it? They're the parents
of all the guppies in the big picture!
How many guppies do you count
all together?
Can you find eight male guppies?
(*Hint:* The males are smaller
than the females.)

It's a Fact:
The name *guppy* comes from
Reverend Robert Guppy — the man who
originally discovered this fish. Guppies
are sometimes called "millionfish"
because there are so many of them.

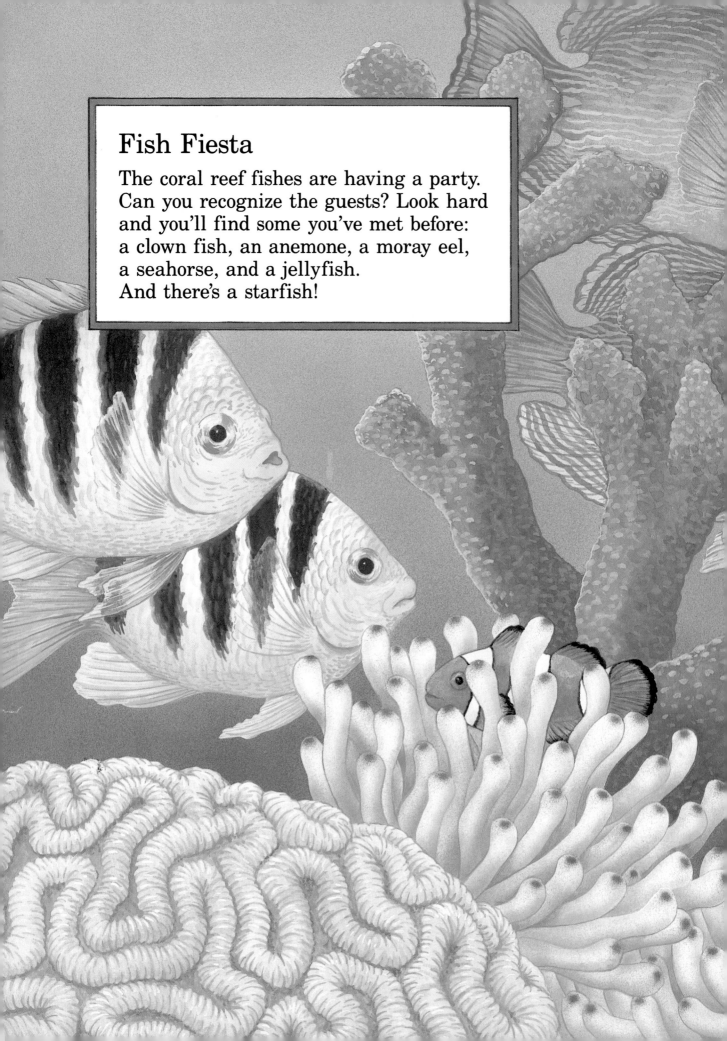

Fish Fiesta

The coral reef fishes are having a party.
Can you recognize the guests? Look hard
and you'll find some you've met before:
a clown fish, an anemone, a moray eel,
a seahorse, and a jellyfish.
And there's a starfish!